THE BEAUTIFUL CHAOS
OF GROWING UP

ALSO BY ARI SATOK

The Architects of Hope

THE BEAUTIFUL

CHAOS

OF GROWING UP

ARI SATOK

The Beautiful Chaos of Growing Up
1st Edition

Copyright © 2018 by Ari Satok
Cover design by Aliisa Lee
Book design by Neeta Patel

ISBN: 978-0-9978435-1-4

For more information about the author, visit *www.arisatok.com*.

DEDICATION

To my incredible family, for their unending love and support.

CONTENTS

IN POSSESSION OF A JOB

EXPERIENCES FROM THE WORKING WORLD

WHEN SALARIES ARE LOW: RETURN TO THE CHILDHOOD BEDROOM

WHEN SALARIES START TO RISE: MOVE-OUT TAKE 2

ON KEEPING IN TOUCH WITH YOUR PARENTS

THE SKILLS OF ADULTING

SKILL 1: LAUNDRY

SKILL 2: COOKING

SKILL 3: PERSONAL FINANCES

A GROWN-UP SOCIAL LIFE

CONCLUSION

INTRODUCTION

When I was a little kid, my friends and I used to sometimes imagine ourselves as adults. Our imaginary adult-selves were always successful; they did whatever our dream jobs were at that moment, lived in beautiful houses, and made life look as effortless as being a grown-up seemed like it should be. As preschoolers, we drew self-portraits of our futures as astronauts and baseball players, rock stars and writers, police officers and pilots, with no idea that the future wasn't that easy.

Follow your dreams, we were told, and life would open up its welcoming doors. No one explained that those doors might not open all that quickly, or that the ones that would open easiest might lead to heartbreak or hardship, to dead ends or roadblocks in the way of our goals. No one said that the path to our dreams might meander its way back through the childhood bedrooms we'd resolved never to return to again, or that sometimes, the dreams we chased might feel as if they were getting further away, not closer. No one said that being an adult might be hard.

When I went away for college, I first started learning some of these lessons of grown-up life. Freshman year was, no doubt, only a junior version of the independence that would follow after college's end, but it was a taste of adulthood nonetheless. I was free in ways I'd never been before — in ways that were exciting and mind-expanding. But I was responsible, too, in ways new and daunting. My choices were finally fully mine; but that meant that my mistakes would be too. No one would tell me when to come home at night, but no one would ask me how my day was when I did.

Four years later, in the summer after graduating from university, living in my first post-college apartment in New York City, I learned even more about growing up. I learned that bank accounts don't refill themselves and that toilet paper rolls don't either. I understood for the first time that adults are sometimes just as confused as children, and that even the ones who seemed to glide through life effortlessly were often treading water beneath the surface. Day by day, I discovered that the path into adulthood was less a smooth road, more a rickety rollercoaster, full of drops and bumps and twists and turns.

This poetry collection was born out of a desire to reflect on that rollercoaster ride into early adulthood and to open up a conversation on what it means to become an adult. It is not autobiographical, though most of the poems are in some way inspired by personal observations, experiences, or feelings.

The poems relate to college and to post-college life — to the years most associated with the beginnings of adulthood. They deal with topics ranging from college roommates to graduation, job searches to apartment hunts, dating to friendship, learning how to cook to learning how to live with love, passion, and adventure. Some of the poems are serious; others are lighthearted. Just as the journey into adulthood evokes the range of human emotions, I thought this collection's poems should too.

When I first started writing these poems, I remember being afraid of the rollercoaster ride that I felt like I was on. I was nostalgic for childhood. I still hoped that becoming an adult would become easier, like those preschool self-portraits made it look.

Slowly, I'm beginning to understand more and more of the things those self-portraits left out: the slog through grad school for the astronaut who one day flies into space, the side-job waiting tables for the writer before her book gets published, the cramped apartment for the musician, desperately waiting to break into the industry. The loop-the-loops on the rollercoaster ride into adulthood where things feel flipped upside down, the hairpin turns where what waits beyond the bend cannot be seen, the steep drops impossible to avoid. But I'm starting to realize that redrawing those self-portraits in all of adulthood's complexity would not make them any less beautiful; that a rollercoaster ride without the drops and the bumps, the twists and the turns, is rarely any fun at all.

GOOD LUCK

THIS POEM IS INSPIRED BY AND MODELED AFTER
RUDYARD KIPLING'S EXCEPTIONAL POEM "IF —"

If you can hold to dreams and aspirations
But know that you have years to live them out;
If you can deal with life's sharp fluctuations
And grasp that some days you will meet with doubt;

If you can ask advice of both your parents
But listen to your heart when it knows best;
If you can learn to budget with forbearance,
But with your money not become obsessed;

If you can online-date without frustration,
And not put too much weight on every text;
If you can work with goals and motivation,
But shed the need to always know what's next

If you can live within a small apartment,
And view it as your castle in the sky;
If you can sort your life into compartments,
But not let its full picture pass you by;

If you can spot a million paths diverging,
But on the choosing, choose to not get stuck
Yours is the world of adulthood emerging,
And so, be on your way to it — good luck!

TIME TO SET SAIL

Sail into adulthood
Ready to catch the wind —
Not to fear it.

PART 1

COLLEGE

DEPARTURE FROM THE
CHILDHOOD HOME

MOVE-OUT DAY

IN THE EYES OF A MATRICULATING FRESHMAN

Hurray, Hurray, today's the day
For years I've dreamed about;
I get to leave my house behind —
I get to now move out!

IN THE EYES OF THAT FRESHMAN'S PARENTS

Hurray, Hurray, today's the day
For years we've dreamed about;
Our house once more will just be ours —
Our son is moving out!

PACKING PROBLEMS

Try to pack your life into a suitcase,
and you'll realize just how much
you cannot fit.

THE THINGS THAT CAN'T BE PACKED

I cannot pack my mother's way of wishing me good night
I cannot pack my grandma's care, my grandfather's delight.

I cannot pack my father's jokes, my best friend's warm embrace
I cannot pack my brother's laugh, my sister's smiling face.

For love cannot be folded; it must stay an outstretched force
And like the Sun that lights the world, it's warmest at its source.

CARRY-ON LUGGAGE

Though many things I leave behind,
For in my bags they can't be packed,
Inside the suitcase of my mind,
In memory, they live intact.

A few such memories sting with pain
But more bring comfort from my past,
And hold great joys inside my brain;
The suitcase of my mind is vast!

ARRIVAL TO CAMPUS

WELCOME TO COLLEGE

Bring an open mind and we will fill it
But in filling it you'll come to understand
That the more you choose to welcome to its chambers,
The more it gains the power to expand.

So we urge you — keep its doors unlocked in welcome.
To the knowledge of the world, proclaim: "Come in!"
Let ideas, in your mind, find homes of comfort
For it's only then that learning can begin.

THROUGH THE EYES OF A FRESHMAN

Into a world of turrets and towers
And quads of great beauty and food at all hours
And white-haired professors with intellect's powers,
A boy came with BIG freshman eyes.

"This campus is heaven," he stated, enchanted,
"I never will take all its blessings for granted,"
The seniors all saw him and watching, they ranted:
"He's in for a jarring surprise

His eyes, like all freshmen's, will one day grow dimmer
For midterms and essays don't sparkle or shimmer;
The feeling he feels will subside."

Said the freshman, "I will not believe in your warning
Four years from today, I'll still wake every morning,
My eyes just as starry and wide."

"It's true," he remarked, "tired eyes can grow blurry
And fill not with joy, but with angst and with worry,
But that will not happen to mine.

For I will remember each day in this setting
To live out my life without ever forgetting
This campus's magical shine."

THROUGH THE EYES OF A PARENT

SOME SMALL ADVICE

Said my parents: "Since we deeply care
we've just a couple thoughts to share
before you settle on a college course.

Some guidance — nothing too defined —
advice of the most laid-back kind
you know there is no way that we'd enforce…"

THE ADVICE

Don't study sociology,
Steer clear of anthropology,
And don't even consider taking psych

Please do not pick a language path,
We'd rather that you don't take math,
And econ — its close cousin — you won't like

Philosophy's a waste of time,
To study English is a crime,
And politics, it's clear, is utter trash

If truth be told, I must admit
That if you take comparative lit
Tuition will feel worse than burning cash

It probably would break Grandpa's heart
To see you study visual art,
Performance, writing, poetry, or dance

And Grandma would be very sad
If you spent all of undergrad
Seduced into a gender studies trance

So if you've thought of any of these
Your Dad and I implore you, please,
To lend a tiny bit of thought instead

To college's most sure-fire bet
That's left no student with regret —
We urge you to at least think of pre-med!

MY FUNDERS

When my parents dropped me off at school
They decided to give me advice
On what classes to take and what friends I should make
And which girls in my hallway looked nice.

Do they not understand all the pressures
Their directions impose on my soul?
Do they not understand this is my life to live?
They're my funders, but that's their whole role.

INTO THE DIRECTOR'S CHAIR

To grow up
Is to grasp
That your parents
Are no longer the directors
Of the play that is your life.

TIME TO MEET MY ROOMMATES

It's time to meet my roommates
Whose names are on my door
Though if I am fully honest
We have somewhat met before.

For I've Facebook-stalked them many times;
I've Googled them as well;
It seems they've done the same for me
As far as I can tell.

So we're fairly well-acquainted
In the realm of cyberspace;
It's time to meet my roommates,
Only this time face-to-face.

FRESHMAN ROOMMATE ADVENTURES:
THE CASE FOR A NOBEL PRIZE

Does the Nobel Peace Prize take in applications?
For if it does, this year I'll send one in
It's true I have not reconciled nations
Nor have I led a nation from within

I haven't ended anybody's hunger
I haven't fought for anybody's rights
I was the same when I was somewhat younger
A Peace Prize never seemed within my sights.

But when my freshman roommates started feuding
About a girl who lived right down the hall
Who was an athlete, beautiful, and brooding,
And sensitive and scholarly and tall,

I knew I could not leave them to their quarrel
I could not let them fight to win one heart
It felt to me both callous and immoral
To idly stand and let a hatred start.

The fear of conflict filled me up with worry,
A fight between them seemed an awful fate,
And so I worked for peace, in righteous hurry —
Before they could, I asked her on a date.

ADVENTURES OF AN
UNDERGRAD

THE ROAD NOT TAKEN: A MODERN ADAPTATION

THIS POEM IS INSPIRED BY AND
MODELED AFTER ROBERT FROST'S
POEM "THE ROAD NOT TAKEN"

Two roads diverged from the campus quad,
One to my dorm; one to frat row,
The choice upon my psyche gnawed,
Faced with what seemed a test of God:
To slumber or to shindig would I go?

The first was lined with cups of beer
And walked upon by girls in heels,
A DJ's beat pulsed loud and clear,
A sports team yelled with raucous cheer
And drank away all of its week's ordeals.

The second was a silent road,
Of any noise completely dead,
Where book-bagged students softly strode
Already in a bedtime-mode,
Prepared to brush their teeth and go to bed.

"I shall be telling this with a sigh
Somewhere ages and ages hence:
Two roads diverged in a quad and I —
I took the one less traveled by,
And that has made all the difference."

THE CHOICE TO CHOOSE

Freedom is not only choosing a path,
But knowing the choice was fully yours to make.

FROM THOSE WHO TOOK
THE ROAD TO THEIR DORMS

TODAYS FOR TOMORROWS

Sometimes it's worth it
To trade todays for tomorrows,
Sometimes it's not,
Life is learning how to know
When is when.

SLIPPERS AND A SNUGGIE

The slippered, Snuggied, cozy nights
In dorm rooms warmed by gentle lights
Where conversation dances its ballet

The patient, quiet, stay-in nights
Companioned by a book's delights
That drive the week's anxieties away

The after-midnight pizza nights
Of late-emerging appetites,
That often, till the break of dawn extend

The tender, loving, warmth-filled nights
Where friendships live and joy ignites:
Those are the nights I wish would never end.

FROM THOSE WHO TOOK
THE ROAD TO FRAT ROW

EXCAVATIONS OF A COLLEGE MINI-FRIDGE

Come take a tour of my mini-fridge,
Behold all its marvelous sights,
Its relics of bygone adventures,
Its remnants of life-changing nights,

Its beers from the first days of frosh week,
Its wings from our first frat event,
Its stains and its spills, large and sticky,
Its vague but unsavory scent,

Its light that for months has been useless.
Its drawers that for days have been jammed,
Its ketchup that long has been empty,
Its freezer, for weeks over-crammed,

Come take a tour of my mini-fridge,
It's a tour I'd be honored to give,
For this fridge, more than all else on campus,
Will reveal to you just how I live.

TOURIST IN THE LIBRARY

Come take a tour of the library,
I've been meaning to see how it looks,
Though I've tried up till now in my schooling,
To avoid all encounters with books.

I've been told it's a magnet for scholars,
I've been told there's a very hot guard,
I've been told that it costs zero dollars
To be given a library card.

I've been told that librarians smile
And there's nothing that can't be looked up,
I've been told there are stacks by the mile
Where some students have even hooked up.

Come take a tour of the library,
It's a tour I'd be honored to lead,
What a thrill it will be to bear witness
To my classmates who actually read.

A GRAND DISCOVERY

Like Columbus when he first observed the New World,
Like Armstrong when he first stepped on the moon,
I, too, beheld a world completely foreign
When I woke up on a Sunday before noon.

FROM EVERYONE TRYING TO STAY
ACADEMICALLY AFLOAT

THE METHODICAL CHAOS
OF SUNDAY NIGHTS

I have to read two Shakespeare plays
And an essay by Montaigne,
And write a six-page paper
On the rule of Charlemagne,

Memorize ten vocab words
And skim through War and Peace,
Write a short reflection
On the late work of Matisse,

Finish thirty lines of code
And a three-page problem-set,
Craft a presentation
On the conflict in Tibet.

What's that you ask dear mother?
When are these assignments due?
Umm…how do I best explain this?
This may not make sense to you…

But they all are due tomorrow
It's a lot, but it's okay;
I've had more before, I promise,
All this work will melt away.

What's that you ask dear mother?
Is this work all close to done?
Umm… I'm not sure how to say this,
But I still have not begun.

What's that you ask dear mother?
Yes tomorrow's what I said.
What's that you ask dear mother?
No, I may not go to bed.

What's that you ask you dear mother?
Yes — I know that isn't smart
What's that you ask dear mother?
Yes — I said I DID NOT START.

So it's time to start in a hurry
For my time is wearing thin;
Distractions — please stay hidden —
My all-nighter must begin!

EVERY COLLEGE STUDENT EVER V. NETFLIX

Your Honor, the guilty defendant
Has robbed me with cunning and guile.
Do not be deceived by his allies
Who sing out his praise at this trial.

It's true — he has stolen no object
Yet his theft is a more heinous crime,
For Your Honor, the heartless defendant
Has stolen my much-needed time.

UNCERTAIN INSTRUCTIONS

"Essay length: ten pages;
Margins: Standard-size;
Typeface: Times New Roman;
And remember to revise!"

That's all Professor told us,
So why was she irate
When my essay was sextuple-spaced
And font size: forty-eight?

IF MIDTERM EXAMS COULD SPEAK

Young man — your pen is spilling
A most incoherent mess,
For instead of writing answers
You are jotting down BS.

I can see your unpreparedness
In your worried, searching eyes;
I can read it in your lengthy nouns
You're hoping will disguise

The fact you chose to party
When you had the chance to cram,
The fact you chose to day-drink
On this day of your exam

The fact you missed nine lectures
And the course had only ten,
The fact I know you'd do the same
If you took this course again.

So young man — feel free to answer me
However you desire,
But know it's no one's fault but yours
When the grade on me's not higher.

GPA IN DANGER

If there is proof there is no God —
No supernatural force —
It's that organic chemistry
Is a mandatory course.

GPA IN PARADISE: REFLECTIONS FROM A SEMESTER IN AUSTRALIA

It's okay — don't be shy; feel free to applaud,
I am Phi-Beta-Kappa of study abroad!

An A in both "Tanning" and "Camping-Trip Planning,"
An A+ in "Using the Beach,"
A– in "Snapchat as Art Form,"
And an A in "Australian Speech"

Yet despite such a rigorous course-load,
There is nothing at all I would change
From the arduous, mind-stretching challenge
That I faced on my year of exchange.

CHALLENGES OF AN
UNDERGRAD

MAJOR MINOR QUESTIONS

Should I double major? Triple major? Major with a minor?
Should I minor with two majors? Is a double minor finer?
Will a minor unrelated to my major be misleading?
Is a minor too connected to my major self-defeating?

Is it best to follow passion or is pragmatism wiser?
Should I seek advice from students? Should I speak to
    my adviser?
Should I panic as my brain feels like it's ready to explode?
I am lost here as I struggle with a MAJOR overload!

THE SPARKS OF STRESS

Stress
is like a forest fire —
fight it when it's small
lest it spreads
to engulf
everything

AS PAPERS GO UNWRITTEN
AND DEADLINES HURTLE BY

THE TREADMILL OF LIFE

I wish there was a button
That could put the world on pause,
Stop the clock's eternal ticking,
Overturn time's natural laws

For my world feels like a treadmill
That is moving far too fast,
And the chance to just get off it
Seems as if it's somehow passed.

So I beg the world: Please help me!
Stop your unrelenting pace;
Give a breather to this runner
In your grueling, painful race.

For no man can run forever,
Tired legs will one day stall;
Do me this one simple favor,
For if you don't stop, I'll fall.

TO THE BOY NEXT DOOR

To the boy next door whose cries I hear,
Who says he wants to disappear,
Whose brain to strange invaders feels on loan

Who sees the world in black and gray,
Whose parents call him every day,
Who wishes hugs could travel through his phone

Who tries to give his hurt a name,
Who drowns in waterfalls of shame,
That are not there, although for him they are

Who's "healthy" though he's always sick,
Whose brain feels like it's lost its stick
Who wonders if a mood can leave a scar

I say to you: You're not alone,
Your burden should not feel your own,
Remind yourself that others hold out light.

For even in the bleakest hour,
Stripped of faith and rid of power,
There always comes the morning after night.

THE PUSH OF THE PRESENT

No yellow brick road that seeks its Oz
Can rid itself of danger;
The future, with its sharpened paws,
Sometimes decides to pounce.

Unknowable, it stays in wait,
A secret, looming stranger,
The worlds it one day will create
It does not preannounce.

The young man, therefore, fears the road
For obstacles will grace it,
And so he sometimes walks it slowed
In hopes they disappear.

But says the Present forcefully,
"Embrace the future — face it
With courage in your heart and not with fear."

TRIUMPHS OF AN
UNDERGRAD

GRADUATION DAY

Grandmas gush with swelling pride that overflows their
　　shrinking frames,
Siblings yawn in boredom, as a Dean reads out a
　　thousand names,
Aunts and uncles wonder why the weather had to be so hot,
Parents clutch their cameras, in the hopes to snap the
　　perfect shot,
While graduates, in gowns and caps, can't help themselves
　　but think:
Let's finish all this pomp and show, so we can go and drink!!!!!

ADVICE FROM THE MAN ON THE STAGE

Carve your own path, said the man on the stage,
Unless there's a good one to take,
Let passion, not wealth, be your trustworthy guide,
Unless there's good money to make.

Dare to be you, said the man on the stage,
Unless you're a pain-in-the-ass,
Care not for grades and for rankings and scores,
Unless you're the top of the class.

Shoot for the moon, said the man on the stage,
Unless you're just fine down on earth,
Measure your life in the love that you give,
Unless other things give you worth.

Go change the world, said the man on the stage,
Unless you will change it for worse,
Always move forward with head held up high,
Unless you'd prefer to reverse.

And now please wake up, said the man on the stage,
For I'm guessing you all just took naps.
Good luck, he then said as the class gave a cheer
And then skyward they all threw their caps.

WELCOME TO THE FUTURE

Basked in graduation's glories
Here we stand upon this stage;
In the books that are our stories
It's come time to turn the page.

College life now stands behind us;
It's official — we've survived!
Lives of meaning — come and find us
For the future's now arrived.

PART 2

LIFE AFTER COLLEGE

THE WORLD WHERE GROWN-UPS LIVE

"Welcome," said the Old Man to the Young Man,
"You have made it to the world where Grown-Ups live,
Just before you settle in and find your bearings,
Here's a little guidance that I often give:

"Stretching forward is a Land of Great Adventure
Filled with love and warmth, with whimsy and delight,
There wait stories of great beauty to be written
No one else but you is qualified to write.

In these stories, though, there won't be only triumph —
Some days failure will accompany success,
In these stories, too, there sometimes will be conflict,
Isolation, inhibition, fear, and stress.

So I urge you — learn to love and laugh and smile
In the goodness of the world, learn to believe,
But I urge you, too, to learn to fail and struggle
And I urge you — learn to cry and hurt and grieve.

For if you can deal with life's highs and its hardships,
When your hair one day like mine has turned to white,
You'll look back upon the Land of Great Adventure
With the knowledge that you traveled through it right."

SEARCHING FOR DIRECTIONS

"I wish there was a map
with directions to the future,"
said the Young Man,
"For then
I wouldn't get lost so many times
along my way."

"What a wonderful shame that would be,"
said the Old Man,
"to live life so afraid of getting lost,
forgetting that sometimes
our greatest discoveries
are ones we were never looking for
in the first place."

IN SEARCH OF A JOB

JOB INTERVIEW

It remains to me a mystery
Why you majored in art history
With a minor in medieval Sufi law,

It appears you took a single course
On commerce of the ancient Norse
And one more on the books of Derrida,

And if your transcript does not lie,
It seems you've studied basic Thai
And metaphysics through the lens of Plato,

You took a class on Robert Frost,
Two times dissected Paradise Lost,
And wrote a paper on the birth of NATO,

And though I'm thrilled that you now know
The early paintings of Van Gogh,
That matters very little in our banks,

You're qualified to write and read —
I'm sure with that you will succeed,
But for this job we have to say no thanks.

THE DOORS THAT AWAIT

You choose
whether to see life's doors
as closed
or as waiting to be opened.

WHEN RESPONSES
DON'T COME QUICKLY

IF HELL EXISTS

If hell exists, I doubt it's full of demons,
No Hades stands in wait upon its shore,
No Devil rules with glee over his kingdom,
No sinners burn in pain forevermore.

If hell exists, I think it looks quite normal,
No long-dead souls, no vast infernal blaze;
Just people in eternal states of waiting
For answers to their sent-out résumés.

REFLECTIONS OF AN INTERN

I'm a photocopy wizard,
I'm a coffee-fetching master,
I'm the savior of my office
From a hole-punching disaster,

I'm the Superman of Staples
I'm a genius at Excel,
I'm a PowerPointing phenom
And I sort mail very well.

I'm a helper like no other,
I'm the office protégé,
And the thing at which I'm very best
Is getting zero pay!

GRAD SCHOOL CONSIDERATIONS

SEVEN YEARS

SENIOR YEAR OF COLLEGE

Seven years of grad school
Sounds like seven years of pain;
All chances of a fun-filled life
Would flush right down the drain.

Every weekend writing papers
Not a soul will ever read,
On a rather meager stipend
Covering less than what I need,

It seems dreary, it seems boring,
It seems difficult indeed;
I won't be swayed; my mind's been made —
No grad school: guaranteed.

THREE MONTHS INTO THE REAL WORLD

Seven years of grad school
Sounds like seven years of bliss
To not even consider it
Would be of me remiss.

I'd be free from endless job hunts,
And I'd take on zero debt,
All my nosy aunts and uncles
Would no longer seem upset.

It seems stable and important,
How'd this never dawn on me?
I won't be swayed; my mind's been made —
I'll get my PhD

DOCTOR MASTERS

They call me Doctor Masters
For I now have ten degrees:
Two MFAs, one MBA,
And seven PhDs

My wall's filled with diplomas,
Though a job I've yet to hold,
But I'm looking for my first one now
At ninety-one years old.

IN POSSESSION OF A JOB

HIDE AND SEEK

Jobs sometimes play hide-and-seek,
but if you keep looking
it's only a matter of time
Until you find them.

HOLY COW

Holy cow — I am employed —
I can't believe my luck!
A real-world contract in my hands;
It seems that gold I've struck.

I've got to sign this contract fast
Before they take it back,
The skills for almost any job
I'm pretty sure I lack.

So find for me a pencil
And, in seconds, I will sign
The paperwork and send it in
So that the job is mine.

I'm excited for employment
All the joy it has in store;
Just remind me for one tiny sec —
What job's this contract for?

Said a Freelance Job to a 9-to-5:
"I fear you don't look well;
I imagine it is suffocating
In your office-prison-cell."

Said the 9-to-5 to the Freelance Job:
"No need to fear for me.
I'm more worried by your meager pay
And your instability."

Said the Freelance Job to the 9-to-5
"Your worry's ill-advised
For my pay is not that meager,
And my freedom's truly prized."

Said the 9-to-5 to the Freelance Job
"It's true that you are free
From the comforts of insurance
And a decent salary."

On they yelled and on they argued
Month by month, then year by year,
Till a thing of which they'd never heard
Appeared and then drew near.

"Why hello there," they both stammered
In a speechless state of awe
Both enraptured by the beauty
Of the thing which they now saw.

"Why hello there," came the warm reply
In its honeyed, silky speech.
"I'm retirement," it said with joy
"I'm what you'll one day reach.

I'm the paradise awaiting
At the end of your careers."
Both the 9-to-5 and Freelance Job
Could not believe their ears

And for the first time both agreed as one
And in unity expressed:
"On one thing there's no arguing:
Retirement's the best."

EXPERIENCES FROM THE
WORKING WORLD

THE LIFE OF A CONSULTANT

I spend most nights with Microsoft Excel,
But our courtship is not going very well,
For the more we've interacted
I've grown less and less attracted
To this partner who makes life a living hell.

THE LIFE OF A STARTUP FOUNDER

Our office has ten beanbag chairs,
A constant stash of gummy bears,
A climbing wall instead of stairs;
But though it seems that no one cares
About our company's affairs,
Somehow, we all are millionaires.

THE LIFE OF AN ARTIST

I was once a secretary
For a businessman named Gary
And a waiter at a restaurant named "Grill."

I am currently a tutor,
Sometimes teaching by computer
For a very wealthy twelve-year-old named Bill.

I've done focus groups and studies,
Taken headshots for my buddies,
Been an Uber driver and a part-time chef.

I've raked leaves and shoveled drivoways,
Back at home, I've now done five stays,
I have babysat and been a soccer ref.

All to float me as a writer,
But if none of this gets brighter
Then perhaps the writing life is not for me.

I may go become a lawyer
With a lucrative employer,
And then claim it's what I always wished to be.

THE LIFE OF A BANKER

I've been holed up in my office
For the past ten lengthy years;
I've missed birthdays of my parents,
I've missed weddings of my peers.

Without sun, I've gone a decade,
Without meals I've gone for days —
But to me it all feels worth it
For I soon might get a raise.

WHEN SALARIES ARE LOW: RETURN TO THE CHILDHOOD BEDROOM

BACK IN THE TWIN BED

Mother's in the kitchen making dinner,
Father's watching baseball on the couch,
Grandma's in the guest room snoring loudly,
Grandpa's acting like a grey-haired grouch,

Skip the Dog is peeing on the carpet,
Jon yaps with his girlfriend on the phone,
And I am on my tiny twin-sized mattress
Wishing that I had not moved back home.

WHEN SALARIES START TO RISE: MOVE-OUT TAKE 2

THE SOUL-SUCKING SEARCH FOR A SUBLET

It's a war without a battlefield
With trenches dug in deep:
To locate an apartment
That's both livable and cheap.

The weaponry's not guns and tanks
But money for the strong,
There are no ethics in this war
Dividing right from wrong.

Instead it's each man for himself,
Objective, only one:
To seek a place in which to live
Until the task's been done.

You gather intel day by day
To seek the upper hand,
Some even send out agents
As a way to understand

The lay of the land, the enemy
From whom you seek to rent,
To draw your own conclusions
On the info that they sent.

Does the kitchen have a working stove?
Is the air conditioning good?
Does the Wi-Fi seem to always work
The way that Wi-Fi should?

Does the shower have good pressure?
Is the lighting good or bad?
Is the place what you envisioned
When you saw its online ad?

* * *

When you finally are satisfied
You launch the great attack.
You make an offer, knowing
That there is no turning back.

And once the offer has been made
All you can do is wait.
Until you find to win this war
You must negotiate.

Which brings the final standoff
That could end in joy or gloom;
The prize, you ask, of this Great War?
An 8-by-7 room.

HOUSEWARMING

Welcome to my living room
That also is my den,
That's also now a B&B
For my college friend named Ben,

That also is my dining room,
That also is my hall,
That's also now a storage room
For my former roommate Paul,

That also is the coatroom,
For my jackets and my shoes,
That also is my bedroom
And a storeroom for my booze,

That's also home to cockroaches
And one enormous mouse —
Welcome to my living room,
That also is my house.

ON KEEPING IN TOUCH
WITH YOUR PARENTS

GREAT EXPECTATIONS: SKYPE EDITION

"I miss you," says your mom on Skype.
"I miss you too," you bluff.
"I wish that we spoke more," she says
"Once weekly's not enough."

"Excuse me!" yells your shaken brain,
"How much more could we speak?
What would we fill the time with
If we spoke three times a week?"

But luckily you catch your thoughts,
Your words are more polite,
"I wish that too," you say with warmth,
"I love you Mom — good night!"

MOMS

Live on your own for just one day,
And you'll realize that moms
Are the ultimate superheroes.

THE SKILLS OF ADULTING

SKILL 1: LAUNDRY

THE WORLD'S MOST VEXING QUANDARY

You stand beset by quandary
When you have not done the laundry
And you realize that you're down to your last shirt.

"I should go do a load today,"
You hear your better judgment say,
"But if I don't nobody will get hurt."

And so you wear a t-shirt twice —
On rare occasions even thrice,
All seems okay; nobody seems to care,

Until you wake one fateful dawn
And grasp that all clean socks are gone,
You wonder: "Can I wear a dirty pair?"

Your mind says no; your heart says "yes!"
"It's my choice in which socks to dress,
And who will notice if they slightly smell?"

So underneath your running shoes
Are socks you secretly reuse,
No one complains; it seems no one can tell.

Yet wearing those unlaundered socks
Unfastens a Pandora's box
A greater quandary waits to one day sprout,

That day arrives — you check your drawer,
You stare upon your clothes-strewn floor,
And realize that your boxers have run out.

And so you say a silent prayer,
You close your eyes and pull your hair,
And wish your laundry would just wash itself,

And dry itself with zero aid,
No shrinking or unwanted fade,
Then end up neatly back upon your shelf.

SKILL 2: COOKING

MASTER CHEF

I'm becoming a master chef,
The best I've ever been,
A culinary artist
With an exceptional cuisine.

My kitchen is a five-star one,
My food: par excellence.
My apartment is the current home
Of a cooking renaissance.

The first thing I have mastered,
Though I do not mean to boast,
Is the fine art, served à la carte,
Of perfectly browned toast.

The second of my specialties
Is a tantalizing rice:
The most refined, of minute kind,
With a taste that does entice.

My menu's last addition
Is a pasta boiled right,
On perfect heat, a joy to eat,
With ketchup on each bite.

I'm proud to say with confidence
My menu's rather bold,
At least compared to other ones
Of which I have been told,

So I'm looking for a sous-chef
If under me you wish to learn,
And I believe in independence
So I'll give you your own turn,

Not once, not twice, but every night,
To emulate my craft,
To follow all my recipes
In my kitchen solely staffed

By you, a future master chef,
As you too become elite,
I promise not to interfere —
I'll just advise and eat.

SKILL 3: PERSONAL FINANCES

A BLEAK AND BARREN BANK ACCOUNT

My bank account is barren as the tundra —
A hostile, rugged place where nothing grows,
I've planted many dollars in its soils,
But it seems as if those soils quickly froze,

For each dollar that I hoped would bloom to many
Instead, all shriveled up and now are gone —
My bank account is barren as the tundra,
But at least the tundra can't be overdrawn.

CAN YOU HELP ME CLIMB THIS MOUNTAIN?

Can you help me climb this mountain?
For I've heard the odds are bleak
That I'll make it without agony
To its distant waiting peak.

I've been climbing it for years now
And I'm feeling very lost,
At the bottom there was little talk
Of this journey's long-term cost.

I am angry, I am tired,
I am caked in tears of sweat:
Think twice, my friend, before you climb
The Mount of Student Debt.

PIGGYBANK NOSTALGIA

Once upon a time I had a piggy bank,
And that was where my savings always went,
They did not go to bonds, nor stocks, nor futures,
Nor student loans, nor ETFs, nor rent.

They did not go to GICs,
Nor RSPs,
Nor hidden fees,
Nor into offshore LLCs,
Nor into funds, nor funds of funds, nor funds of funds of funds
    of funds,
Nor CDOs, nor fancy clothes,
Nor cars, nor bars, nor IPOs,
Nor health insurance, car insurance, debt insurance,
    pet insurance, doctor visits, drug prescriptions,
    online magazine subscriptions, movie passes,
    yoga classes, WiFi, cable, brand new glasses

ALL THE EVER-CLIMBING COSTS OF LIFE

Once upon a time I had a piggy bank,
And that was where my savings always went;
Once upon time I had a piggy bank —
With that and nothing more I was content.

COMPLICATED

Life starts simple
And ends simple.
In the middle, though,
We find ways to make it complicated beyond belief.

A GROWN-UP
SOCIAL LIFE

ASLEEP BEFORE MIDNIGHT

I've gained the right to drive a car,
To patronize my local bar,
To buy my college friends some beers,
To join a jury of my peers,
To sign a lease and pay my rent,
To cast my vote for president,
And most of all I've gained the right
To go to bed by ten at night.

TO PARTY OR NOT TO PARTY

I heard about this party
From my cousin's roommate Marty
Who was told about it by his cousin Ken,

Who was texted by his cousin
In a GroupMe of a dozen
With the message that the party was at ten.

I was told I should not get there
When Ken's cousin was not yet there
Because Ken was gonna wait for him to go,

I was also told that Marty,
Who had told me of the party,
Would ensure that Ken was there before he'd show.

This etiquette perplexed me,
And when Marty said he'd text me,
I said, "Why don't we just meet there right at ten?"

He responded very surly,
"We can't show up there that early,
And there's no way that we're going without Ken."

At which point I could not take it,
So I said, "I cannot make it
An emergency's come up that's flipped my plan,"

I then changed out of my flannel
Searched my favorite YouTube Channel,
And a simpler night of YouTube clips began.

IN SEARCH OF LOVE

SWIPE RIGHT

Grandpa — how did you and Grandma meet?
Did you meet her at a school dance and then sweep her
   off her feet?
Did you lend her an umbrella in a rainstorm on the street?
Did you send a box of chocolates and then ask her on a date?
Did you see her on the streetcar, knowing marriage was
   your fate?
Did you spot her walking on the beach beneath the moon's
   bright light?
Or did you see her on your phone and know you should
   swipe right?

OUR DEAR BUDDY DAN

My friend is getting married, and I'm nervous,
As I stand here as the best man at his service,
Will this wedding day transform him?
To the wedded-life conform him?
Is he really certain that he will prefer this?

Will he still hold to the values that defined him?
What he once found fun will we need to remind him?
Will the closest friend I've ever known
Wake up tomorrow fully-grown
With his childhood completely left behind him?

Will he cease to let us call him by his nicknames?
Will he snap if we make jokes about his old flames?
Will he keep on playing PS4?
Will he road-trip with us anymore?
Will he still come out to dive bars to watch sports games?

Will he cross the bridge from child to man
To a life mapped by a constant plan?
Will he have a kid, or buy a house
In his newfound life as Stacey's spouse?
What will happen to our dear, dear buddy Dan?

QUESTIONS FROM MY GREAT AUNT

My great-aunt asks me, "When will you get married?"
Then she asks me, "When will you find work?"
So I ask my great-aunt one less prying question,
"When will you stop being such a jerk?"

GROWN-UP PRESSURES

Some days,
When everyone is yelling at me to be an adult,
All I want to do
Is go back
And be a kid.

CHILDHOOD NOSTALGIA

I WISH I WERE A CHILD AGAIN

I wish I were a child again,
Returned to preschool life,
Played Little League,
No work fatigue,
Or stress to find a wife.

I wish I were a child again,
With snack time twice a day,
Took class called gym,
Was small and slim,
And starred in my school play.

I wish I were a child again,
Read only picture books,
Wore Velcro shoes,
Ignored the news,
And cared not for my looks.

But though I'm not a child now,
So says my year of birth,
I'm childlike,
A grown-up tyke,
For all that that is worth.

ONE LAST TIME

My pediatrician tells me
I'm too old to keep on seeing him,
"It's time," he says,
"To find another doctor
With no stickers at reception,
With no waiting room with games and toys,
No animals
Alive in paint upon the walls,
That smile, saying, "All will be okay."

I tell him I will search for one
And find a place
Where moms don't watch
Their children bravely get their shots,
Where no one stands on tippy-toes
To measure every extra inch,

But we both know
That I won't search;
Instead,
I'll call him pleadingly
When my next check-up cannot wait
And ask him if he'll let me
Stay a kid
For one last time.

THE KIDS' TABLE

THERE sit the children — allowed to be slobs —
Who don't talk of taxes or exes or jobs,

With seats unassigned for they all will be fine
No matter the neighbors with whom they will dine.

THERE sit the children who do not complain:
We're too far, we're too close, we've been shafted again,

With no grudges to bear and no feuds to conceal
And no checks still to write based on feelings they feel.

THERE sit the children with fingers and fries
With looks of contentment affixed in their eyes,

And they smile and laugh without worry or care;
Oh how I wish I could once more sit there!

EYES TOWARD
THE FUTURE

AN ADULT'S FOOLISH GAME

Children
Don't endlessly fear the roads they take
And the ones they pass up.
Worry
Is an adult's
Foolish game.

THE NEVER-ENDING LADDER

Life appears to me a ladder
Stretching upward without end
With the giants further upward
Yelling downward to ascend.

"We have made it," they all bellow,
Of their happiness they preach.
"Life is better here young fellow —
In this land you'll one day reach."

So I grip the ladder tightly
For I do not want to fall,
And I keep my feet in motion
For I do not want to stall.

But the closer that I get
To where I thought the giants were,
The higher that it seems they get —
An ever-distant blur.

THE PLACE WHERE FUTURES WAIT

There is a place where futures wait,
Life's happy endings side-by-side,
But plots do not stand crafted yet
To which those endings can be tied,

And so the young man must decide —
Are endings worth their messy plots?
Are summits worth their arduous climbs
Or are they better left as thoughts?

RACING TO TOMORROW

The young look to their futures as a race
The fastest to their goals the winning few
And so they run at a most rapid pace
With nothing but their finish lines in view
It seems that others run beside them, too,
But on they run; no finish line arrives —
Just further track to fill their hurried lives.

ACHING FOR TOMORROW

I'm an author one submission from my opus,
I'm a singer one performance from my tour.
I'm an actress one audition from my breakthrough,
I'm a doctor one invention from a cure.

I'm a banker one investment from my riches,
I'm a playwright one connection from a play.
I'm a runner one more practice from a medal,
I'm tomorrow, though I can't escape today.

A MAN AND HIS SHRINK

Said a man to his shrink,
"I'm beginning to think
That I can't measure up to my goals."

Said the shrink to the man,
"You most certainly can;
What you do is within your control."

Said the man to his shrink,
"In my worries I sink,
For I feel like I'm falling behind."

Said the shrink to the man,
"In the view of whose plan
Do these worries and doubts claim your mind?"

"Is it you," said the shrink
"Or your parents who think
That your journey is somehow too slow?"

"Or perhaps," the shrink said
"All the fear in your head
Comes from some other person you know?

Let me tell you, young man,
Life is more than a plan
To be realized and marked with a check,

So discard all the worry,
Abandon your hurry,
And relish the path that you trek."

WALK

Better to walk slowly
To where you want to go
Than to run quickly
In the wrong direction.

LIFE IS A LONG STORY

Life is a long story,
And no good author
Puts all of his most beautiful moments
In the opening chapter.

THE OPENING CHAPTER

When you're learning how to stand, at first you tumble,
When you're learning how to walk, at first you crawl,
When you're learning how to run, at first you stumble,
When you're learning how to bike, at first you fall.

There is no way to avoid the painful scratches,
But remember that in time they disappear,
So go trip your way through adulthood's first patches
As you walk along the Grown-Up Life's frontier.

NO SMALL TASK

If growing up was easy
It wouldn't take so long
To do.

INVISIBLE EVOLUTIONS OF THE SOUL

Nobody wakes up one morning
All grown up,
Maturity tends to sneak up on us,
Hidden in the invisible evolutions of the soul
We wake to each day
Teaching us
How to carry our own lives,
Heavy as they are,
And how to find the strength
To carry the lives of others, too.

THE WAYS I'VE GROWN

Mom and Dad, come visit me; observe the ways I've grown,
See the adult ways I live and all the adult things I own.

I have paintings on my walls now; I have carpet on my floor,
I have all the dishes I could need, and then I have some more,

I shop on sale,
I cook with kale,
My laundry's always done,

I exercise,
Own seven ties,
And find the opera fun,

I understand insurance plans and never miss my rent,
I file taxes early and in dating I'm content.

And most of all, I now can deal with stress and strain and strife.
Mom and Dad, come visit me, and see my adult life!

CONCLUSION

The first summer after I graduated university, a movie called *Boyhood* came into theaters. It was a coming-of-age story, tracking the life of its protagonist, Mason Evans Jr., as he aged through childhood and adolescence. The movie quickly gained widespread attention on the basis of its uniqueness; it had been filmed over the course of 12 years. Each year, the cast would gather together, and, for one week, shoot the next scenes from the film. Their onscreen aging was their off-screen aging; Mason's evolution was informed by the evolution of the real-life actor who played him. For every year of his life, there were corresponding scenes in the film, and what emerged was a cinematic timeline of boyhood and youth.

The film was striking for a number of reasons but what struck me most was what it revealed about growing up. With every on-screen jolt one year forward, a new Mason would appear, so remarkably alike to the Mason of before, yet so remarkably different at the very same time. In Mason, from one scene to the next, lived the contradiction of getting older — the way in which it is at once gradual and sudden, painstakingly slow and lightning fast.

As I've started my journey into adulthood, I've felt this contradiction that Mason's aging in the film so beautifully captures — this mix of fast-paced transformation and imperceptible evolutions of character and conduct that only time reveals. To grow up is both to hurtle into the future, and to grasp just how long it will take to get to its furthest destinations. It is speed and slowness, anxiety and exhilaration, constancy and change.

I call myself an adult today, the same way I did at 21 during that first summer after university, the same way I did at 18, watching as my parents' car drove away from my college campus. It's obvious these versions of me are radically different from one another. And the versions of me I'll go on to become may be even more unalike. But all of these versions of myself, in different ways, share what I think makes adults adults — an understanding of their lives as their own; their futures theirs to shape.

To take responsibility for one's own life is a scary thing. It's why so many of my friends and I still cherish our pampered visits home, those temporary abdications of our responsibilities as the CEOs of our lives. Dinner waits on the table; laundry magically gets done; life momentarily reverts to the ease of childhood. But young adulthood's challenge, its often uncomfortable difficulty, is what makes it meaningful. Ease is enjoyable; challenge is fulfilling.

In the years to come, I'm sure that sense of challenge won't suddenly disappear. Life will sometimes be heavy — decisions, sometimes stressful. There will be more questions than answers. There will be moments of uncertainty and confusion. But in those questions and confusion and uncertainty, there will be a grand adventure. And in that adventure lies the beautiful chaos of growing up.

ON THE WAVES OF ADULT WATERS

There will still be days when life feels overwhelming,
When its challenges are heavy ones to bear,
When its tests and trials loom like fearsome monsters,
When its outcomes and its endings seem unfair.

There will still be days when life's paths look unfriendly,
When its ladders to success stand extra steep,
When new canyons block the roads you've always travelled,
And to cross them you must find the nerve to leap.

On these days, you'll sometimes wish to flee for childhood,
For it's calmer and it's safer on that shore
Than it is out on the waves of adult waters
With their swells and tides no person can ignore.

But embrace the stormy waters you now travel,
For in calmness, very few adventures start;
Steer with courage and an adult's hard-earned wisdom,
Though remember to maintain a child's heart.

And when one day you have made it through the tempest,
When the currents slow, the waves recede and fade,
You will smile that you looked out on those waters
And then chose to journey onward unafraid.

ACKNOWLEDGMENTS

This book project started in the summer of 2014. It's been a long road since then, filled with so many people who have inspired and encouraged me.

To everyone who helped in this book's editing process, thank you for all the great advice.

To Neeta Patel, my exceptional interior designer, and to Aliisa Lee, my remarkable cover designer, thank you for creating for my poems such a perfect home in which they now live.

To my Mom and Dad, thanks for being so supportive of me in all of my endeavors; I never forget how lucky I am to have parents so fully behind me as I try to chart a less than conventional path.

To Josh and Jordy, thanks for your constant advice whenever I needed it throughout this book project. And more importantly, thanks for being the greatest siblings anyone could ask for.

To my amazing friends, thank you for always believing in me, and for all the glorious times together.

To the countless writers and storytellers who inspire me with your work, thank you for constantly showing me what beautiful words can do.

And to everyone who has ever shared with me a kind word, a message of encouragement, a gesture of appreciation, thank you so much. You don't how much those little sparks of inspiration mean to anyone daring to raise their creative voice in the world.

To become an adult, as this book acknowledges, is full of challenges. But, in my mind, there's no better way to overcome these challenges than with the love and support of so many wonderful people cheering you on.